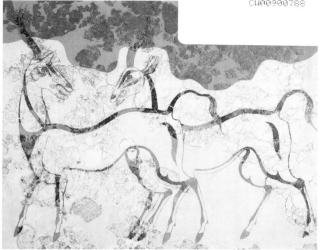

# SANTORINI

A full travel guide with 140 colour photographs which will
introduce you to the island 's history, art and folklore.
It guides you round archaeological sites
and others sights, and takes you over
routes on the island.

EDITIONS: HAITALIS

EDITING AND DTP : BARRAGE LTD

TEXTS: REGINA MOYSTERAKI

ENGLISH TRANSLATIONS: COX AND SOLMAN

ART EDITING: FOTINI SVARNA

PRINTING: LITHOGRAFIKI S.A

PHOTOGRAPHS: HAITALIS PUBLISHING Co. ARCHIVE

COLOUR SEPARATIONS:HAITALIS

# CONTENTS

# An Introduction to Santorini

p.6
*Fira, capital of Santorini, crowns the brow of the cliff on the side facing the caldera.*

p. 7
*One of the many churches on Santorini:the blue cupolas and white belltowers of these buildings seem to be competing with the colours of the sea and sky.*

Santorini is one of the most southerly islands in the Cyclades. It lies between Ios and Anafi, has an area of 96 square kilometres, and its permanent population numbers 11,381. It is situated 130 nautical miles from Piraeus and 70 nautical miles from Crete. The coastline measures 69 kilometres in length, while the island itself is 18 kilometres long (from Cape Mavropetra in the north to Cape Exomytis in the south) and between two and six kilometres wide. The capital of the island is Fira, and Athinios is its port.

The semicircular shape of the island today is the result - as, indeed, was the creation of the island itself - of the eruptions of a volcano, which was active as far back as prehistoric times (see Volcanic Activity). On the west side, where the volcano is located, Santorini is steep and rocky. The west coast ends in a steep precipice which plunges into the caldera, a circular lagoon-

like body of water that measures 32 square miles and is 300 to 400 metres deep.

pp. 8-9

*The steep walls of the caldera, with towering rocks and sharp contrasts between the shades of black and red in the rock strata,*

The cliffs surrounding the caldera, which range in height from 150 to 300 metres, consist of horizontal, parallel bands of red and black rock and lava that were formed during repeated eruptions. Perched on the rim of the cliffs are the island's main towns, Fira and the pretty village of Oia.

The landscape of the outer side of Santorini is very different from the cliffs overlooking the caldera. In the centre of the island, from north to south, are the limestone massifs of Megalo Vouno, Mikros Profitis Ilias, Profitis Ilias and Gavrilos. The highest of these mountains, Profitis Ilias, has a summit only 556 metres above sea level. The ground stretching towards the east coast is flat

*create a magical atmosphere further enhanced by the white houses of Fira.*

and fertile. This is where the towns of Pyrgos, Emborio, Karterado and Finikia are situated, with the beaches of Kamari, Perissa and Monolithos, which have pebbles or black sand.

The climate of Santorini is pleasant even in the summer, which is comparatively cool. The northeasterly winds which prevail in the summer months help to keep the temperature down.

*p. 10*

*A miniature cable railway links Fira and Mesa Yialos. The view from above over the caldera and the volcano of Santorini is of incomparable beauty.*

The island's soil, thanks to its volcanic origins, is unusually fertile. Its farm produce has long been famous for quality and taste. The most prized of these products is the wine of Santorini. Apart from the brusco and vinsanto vintages, the island also produces a variety called 'nychteri', a name derived from the way in which it is made. 'Nychteri' is made from unpressed grapes piled in

the vats overnight. The juice seeps from them very slowly, squeezed out by their own weight.

Apart from vines, the island also favours tomatoes, small perhaps but exceptionally tasty. The locals made tomato paste from them to store for the difficult days of winter. They also grew barley, cucumbers and yellow peas. The peas, of a special variety, are used to make 'fava', a kind of paste eaten with olive oil, chopped onions and lemon juice. Another of the island's important economic resources is layer of tufa beneath the surface of its soil, at some points reaching up to 30 to 40 metres thick. Large quantities of this material, which has in-sulatory properties, are still exported and much of it was used in the construction of the Suez Canal. Today, the agricultur-

*p. 11*

*A typical beach on Santorini, with the harsh volcanic rocks contrasting strikingly with the calm of the sea.*

al production of the island is much lower than it was in the past - with the exception of viticulture - and the islanders are mostly engaged in occupations related to tourism.

Santorini in recent years has developed into a summer holiday resort for thousands of Greeks and foreigners. Its important archaeological sites and its stunning beauty, which is mainly a function of its extraordinary landscape, attract tourists from all over the world every summer.

*pp. 12-13*

*The unique landscape of the island, its history and the traditional life-style of the islanders attract thousands of visitors from all over the world each year.*

# Myth and History

## VOLCANIC ACTIVITY

Over the centuries, the islanders have given their home various names. It has been called Strongyle (the Round One), Kalliste (the Beautiful One), Philotera, and Santorini. In the 20th century, many people have linked its turbulent past with the tragic fate of the legendary continent of Atlantis. Scholars and scientists, geologists and archaeologists, have treated it with wonder and interest as they tried to piece together its long story from the information available to them.

But let us see how its tragic history has unfolded. Mythology tells us that Santorini was created from a lump of earth from far-off Libya. History, complemented by geology and archaeology, gives us a series of mind-shattering facts related to the creation and evolution of this amazing place, which the French geologist, F. Fouque, rightly called the "Pompeii of the Aegean". But in order for us to follow Santorini's progress through the ages, we should first try to sketch a picture of what Greece looked like hundreds of millions of years ago.

In the beginning, the Greek earth was covered by water. Gradually and after vast upheavals in the bowels of the planet, sections of dry land rose up above the water some 30,000,000 years ago and

*p. 15*
*View of Fira and Mesa Yialos, off which cruise ships can drop anchor.*

created Aegeis. This was a single land mass stretching from the Ionian Sea to Asia Minor and the south coast of Crete. The geological shifts in the earth's crust continued. With the passage of time, the sea penetrated the interior of Aegeis, breaking it into pieces. Part of it - what is today the Aegean Sea - sank, leaving only its mountain peaks which still protrude above the surface.

In the situation now occupied by Santorini, only a rocky islet remained, corresponding today to the district of Profitis Elias and Pyrgos. From that time on, the subsequent evolution of the island into its present shape was the result of the long-term activity of volcanoes, which made their appearance in the region as early as 26,000,000 years ago. Thus, about 2,000,000 years ago, the first volcanic craters began to form southwest of Profitis Elias, Over time, the craters broke through the surface of the sea and then united to form what is now Akrotiri. Later volcanic activity created other craters to the north of

*p. 17*

*The volcano of Santorini was the main factor behind the creation of the island. Today, the fumes that emerge from the crater give visitors a tiny hint of what must have happened at the time of the eruption.*

the already existing island. The volcanic cones and the rocky islet predating them slowly began to fuse together thanks to the matter that spilled out during eruptions, eventually forming a single island, which because of its shape was called, as Herodotus tells us, Strongyle or 'the Round One'.

What did Strongyle really look like, one wonders, in those days? Scientists have concluded that it must have been an imposing volcanic cone, with a height of about 1,000 metres and a diameter of 14 to 15 kilometres. There would have been a crater at the top of the cone and other smaller ones along its sides. Lava would burst from the craters, to flow bubbling hot down to the sea. With time the volcano became extinct and after thousands of years plants and animals began to live on the island.

The fertile soil of Santorini seems to have attracted the first settlers during the fifth millen-nium BC (in the Neolithic period), as we can see in the finds from the site at Akrotiri. In the Early and Middle Bronze Age (3200-2000 and 2000-1550 BC) settlements began to develop on sites other than Akrotiri.

*p. 18*
*View of Nea Kameni, where the crater of the volcano is located.*

The inhabitants were mostly farmers, but they also traded with other places by sea. Trade grew still further during the Late Bronze Age - in the period around 1550-1500 BC - when the Minoans of Crete were masters of the Aegean and had a decisive influence on the civilisation of Thera. But in about 1500 BC that civilisation suffered a mortal blow when the volcano erupted, ultimately resulting in the eradication of the human settlements on Santorini.

## THE CHRONICLE OF THE CATASTROPHE

Let us cast our minds back, then, to the middle of the 16th century BC. 'Written documents, which could tell us exactly what happened, do not exist.

p. 19

*Nea Kameni was formed from the material spewed out during eruptions of the volcano in the modern period. The black masses of lava give us some idea of what the whole area must have looked like after the terrible eruption of 1500 BC.*

Historians try, from other evidence within their grasp, to piece together the picture of the dreadful catastrophe that befell Santorini.

Earthquakes were always a common occurrence in the region. One especially cata-strophic earth-quake must have triggered the volcano, and it awoke. The houses, some with two storeys and some with three, were partially destroyed. Most of the residents abandoned the island in panic, and it seems that, forewarned by some worrying sign, they did not return.

They took whatever valuables they had with them: the dig at Akrotiri has unearthed no ob-jects of any worth, no jewels, seals or other valuables, no skeletons of humans or animals, apart from that of a pig. Today, one can see traces of heavy objects having been moved im-printed on the ash and tufa. This tells us that some of the inhabitants must have stayed on the island until the vol-cano started to erupt. Even these people, however, since their skeletons have not been found, must have left Thera at some point. Professor Spyri-don Marinatos, who

*p. 21*
*View of Oia. The bulk of Mt Profitis Ilias can be seen in the background.*

was in charge of the excavations at Akrotiri, called these people troglodytes, people who lived among the ruins. Christos Doumas, another archaeologist, believes that they formed a team who were attempting to repair the damaged buildings. The length of time that elapsed between the earthquake and the eruption of the volcano is not known. However, it must have been at least a year. Scientists have deduced this from the fact that some seeds left in the ruined houses after the earthquake

had begun to sprout when the first ash started to fall from the erupting volcano.

The whole island was buried under a thick layer of tufa, which at many points is over thirty metres deep. Huge chunks of basalt were thrown from the crater with such force that many of the houses at Akrotiri were struck by them. The intensity of the explosion must have been tremendous. The material thrown up from inside the cone of the volcano, which was in the centre of the island, appears to have created a huge vacuum inside. The crust of the earth collapsed and the larger central portion of Strongyle was sucked down into the vacuum. Eighty-three square kilometres of earth vanished into the abyss of the crater, which had a depth of 800 m. The sea rushed in and flooded the spot, which had once been dry land. All that remains of Strongyle today is Santorini, Therasia and Aspronisi. This catastrophe of truly inconceivable proportions must have been accompanied by enormous tidal waves which, according to the experts, could have reached a height of 210 metres at the start before slamming against the shores of the Aegean with indescribable fury. The 'three-day night' of Heracles and myths from Attica, the Argolid, the Aegean islands and Lycia are probably nothing more than echoes from the memories of people who had lived through this incredible disaster and who were attempting to wrest some meaning out of the ensuing phenomena. For days on end, darkness must have reigned and day was turned into night. The volcanic ash that spewed forth must have fallen on the earth within a huge circumference, charring all vegetation.

As a means of understanding the dimensions of

the devastation that occurred, we can take the 1883 eruption of Krakatoa, in the strait of Sunda between Java and Sumatra. In that eruption, 22.8 square kilometres of the island were blown up and then sank to a depth of 200-300 metres. Witnesses' reports are mind-boggling, the scale of the disaster inconceivable. For several months the ports near Krakatoa were unapproachable by ships. Ash covered the sky for a distance of 150 kilometres, and there were tidal waves 30 metres in height which struck many parts of Sumatra with unbelievable force and swept away an entire city on nearby Java. An estimated 30,000 people were killed. With this information in mind, we can perhaps form a picture, albeit blurred, of what happened when prehistoric Strongyle blew up in what was, as far as we know, the most violent explosion in the history of the earth: for example, the crater left after the eruption was four times the size and depth of that of the island of Krakatoa.

The phenomena that accompanied the explosions and sinking of the cone of the volcano and the finding of pumice during his excavations at Amnissos in Crete, in 1932, led Professor Spyros Marinatos to formulate a new theory. According to him, the decline of the Minoan civilization around 1500 BC was the result of the blow dealt by the frightful consequences of the eruption of the volcano on Santorini. The tidal waves must literally have shaved the shores of Crete, where stood not only the palace of Cnossos but also those of Mallia and Zakro along with many other important towns. The interior of the island must have been badly damaged by the strong seismic tremors which shook the whole region. This theory has not been accepted unreservedly because the dating of samples of Minoan

pottery places the decline of Minoan civilization at least fifty years after the eruption of Santorini. For many scholars, this means that the Minoans were brought down by some other cause. Nevertheless, what seem almost certain is that the effect of the eruption of the Thera volcano on all of the Aegean, including Crete, must have been horrendous.

Between 1500 BC and 1950, the volcano of Santorini came alive on a total of fourteen occasions, erupting with varying degrees of intensity. The first eruption was in 197/196 BC, and it led to the formation of Palaia Kammeni, the island which the ancient Greeks called Hiera. In 1573, fresh sections of dry land appeared, joining with Mikri Kammeni and forming the volcano as we see it today: Nea Kameni.

# THE ATLANTIS QUESTION

Santorini has often been connected with Atlantis, the legendary continent that sank to the bottom of the sea while it was at its zenith. The mystery surrounding the destruction of the one and the disappearance of the other has preoccupied scientists for generations.

The starting-points for the debate about Atlantis are the references to be found in Plato's dialogues *Timaeus* (21E-25D) and *Critias* (108E-121C). According to the account given in *Timaeus*, when the Athenian law-giver Solon visited Egypt (c. 590 BC), he was told the story of Atlantis by a priest at Sais: the place had been "a great and wonderful state which ruled over the other islands" and owed its power to the civilisation that had evolved there.

pp. 24-25

*The islet of Nea Kameni emerged in the middle of the caldera of Santorini in 1573. On it, one can visit the crater of the volcano.*

The kingdom consisted of two islands, the "larger" and the "smaller", and there were ten cities. Of these, only two are mentioned more specifically: the "metropolis" and the "royal city". The people of Atlantis had launched an attack on Athens 900 years before the time Solon had his talk with the priest, and by that time they were already masters of many other lands, from Libya to Egypt and Europe. But the Athenians defeated them, and liberated all the lands that Atlantis had conquered. Later, Atlantis suffered a terrible earthquake and a flood, sinking in its entirety beneath the waves and making the sea around it shallow, muddy and impossible to sail across. In *Critias* we find even more information about Atlantis: it had been founded by Poseidon, we are told, and Plato describes its monarchs, its administration, its social classes, the occupations and customs of its inhabitants, the climate, the terrain, the architecture and the facilities provided by its harbour. The narrative continues with the decline of the island's culture and the decision taken by the gods to destroy it, but breaks off suddenly at the point where Zeus has summoned the gods and is about to address them.

The finds from the excavations at Akrotiri, which indicate the presence of a high level of civilisation, its violent cessation, and the fact that both catastrophes took place at about the same time, have led many scholars to conclude that the lost Atlantis was none other than Santorini. However, Professor Marinatos gave a different interpretation of the myth. According to him, Atlantis should really be identified with Minoan Crete, since the disasters that befell Crete after the eruption were fatal to its further development. Furthermore, the topography and shape of Atlantis, as described by the ancients, greatly resemble those of the plateau of Messara in Crete. Perhaps Crete was the "larger" island, the "royal city", while Santorini, with which Crete had ties, would have been the "Metropolis" or "smaller" island. Over the centuries, as the myth was told and retold, it is very likely that the events underwent subtle changes. Thus the destruction of a civilisation, the Minoan, was attributed to the sinking of the island - but the island that blew up and subsequently sank was a large part of Santorini, not Crete. Nevertheless, the question still remains: was there such a place as Atlantis? Or did Plato, perhaps wishing to instruct his compatriots on the consequences that can arise when mortals are lacking in respect for the gods, himself fabricate the myth of the lost continent, drawing on memories of the facts about the real destruction of Santorini?

## A BRIEF OVERVIEW OF THE ISLAND'S HISTORY FROM 1300 BC TO MODERN TIMES

After the eruption of the volcano in about 1500 BC, the island remained uninhabited for some two centuries. Traces of human life have been found, dating to the late 13th century BC. According to Herodotus, the Phoenicians

were so enthralled by the beauty of Santorini that they settled there and gave it the name Calliste (which means most beautiful). There is a myth that the first colonist of the island was called Membliarus, who settled there with some of the companions of Cadmus. (Cadmus was the son of the Phoenician king Agenor, and he had undertaken the search for his sister Europa, abducted from her home by Zeus in the guise of a bull. During his travels, he visited Santorini and founded a small colony there.)

Tradition also relates that later the Minyans from Boeotia established a settlement on Thera. Herodotus, however, informs us that at the end of the 12th century BC the Dorians arrived from Sparta, led by King Theras, who was the son of Autesion, a descendant of Cadmus and great-grandson of Oedipus. Although he was a Theban hero, Theras lived in Sparta as regent and guardian of his young nephews, Procles and Eurysthenes. When they came of age, Theras left Sparta and sailed to Santorini, where he settled. Ever after, the island was called Thera in his honour.

By the 9th century BC, the island was a thoroughly Dorian colony, whose centre was at Ancient Thera on a fortified position on Mesa Vouno ('Middle Mountain'). During this time, Santorini, along with the coastline of southeastern mainland Greece, Crete, Melos and Cyprus, constituted a bridge unifying East and West. True descendants of the Spartans, the Therans created a closed society which permitted few influences from outside, and those only from residents of neighbouring islands. However, the location they had chosen was so crucial to sea communication that, although the island did not

*p. 28*

*Part of the ship mural which ornamented room 5 in the West House of the prehistoric settlement at Akrotiri.*

share the history of the other islands in the Cyclades group, it nevertheless could not remain completely unaffected by what was going on around it.

Thus, by the late 9th or early 8th century BC, Thera, Crete and Melos were the first places to adopt the Phoenician alphabet as a way of writing the Greek language. In the 7th and 6th centuries BC, the island began to have contact with other regions of Greece: first with Crete and Paros, and later with Attica, Corinth, Rhodes and Ionia in Asia Minor. Its inhabitants subsisted on a frugal diet, consisting solely of what the island could produce. They were not concerned much with either trade or shipping. The first people to leave the island did so in 630 BC, founding a colony on the north coast of Africa called Cyrrhene. They only resorted to this after a long period of drought, which ravaged the island for seven years.

By the 6th century BC Thera was minting its own currency. During the Classical era (5th and 4th centuries BC), it was content to remain on the sidelines. It was subjugated by the Persians and the mint ceased functioning. During the Peloponnesian War, Thera allied itself with the Spartans. In 426/425 BC it came under the control of the Athenians and was forced to join the Delian League. When the Macedonians gained supremacy over the rest of Greece, Thera too followed. Likewise, during the Hellenistic period, it was ruled by the Ptolemies of Egypt, who valued its strategic location enough to found a harbour called Eleusis there. They also transformed the Mesa Vouno district, where Ancient Thera was located, into a major base for the military operations they were conducting in the Aegean. Under Roman domination, after 146 BC, Thera fell into total ob-

*p. 31*

*A kouros of the sixth century BC, found at Exomyti and known as the Apollo of Thera (National Archaeological Museum, Athens).*

scurity. Within the vast stretches of the Roman Empire it was nothing more than one of the scores of inconsequential Aegean islands. During the Byzantine era, it acquired a modicum of political and military significance. It was incorporated into the Byzantine Empire and belonged to the 'Theme' of the Aegean. Christianity must have reached Thera in the 3rd century. By the end of that century there were already converts to the new religion on the island. By the start of the 4th century there was an organized church on Santorini, which is referred to as the Bishopric of Thera, the first bishop having been Dioscurus (342-344). It was one of eleven bishoprics that were subject to the Cathedral of Rhodes, and it ranked fifth in seniority. The prosperity of the Christian community on Thera in the Early Christian era is borne out by the existence of three old basilicas. One of them was erected at Ancient Thera on Mesa Vouno and must have been dedicated to the Archangel Michael. The second was built on the site of the present Byzantine church of Piskopi Gonia. It was on its ruins that in 1081-1118 the emperor Alexius I Comnenus founded the church of Our Lady of Gonia or Piskopi, which may have been the main church of a monastery. The third basilica was erected at Perissa where the Byzantine church of St Irene stands today.

In 1153, for the first time, we find mention of the island in the writings of the Arab geographer Edris under a new name, Santorini. This seems to have been given by the Crusaders, from the chapel of St Irene (Santa Irini - Santorini), which some scholars place at Perissos, others on Therasia.

When Constantinople fell to the knights of the Fourth Crusade in 1204, Santorini and many of the other islands in the Aegean passed into the hands of Marco Sanudo. He founded what was called the Duchy of Naxos (or of the Archipelago) and later ceded Santorini and Therasia - as a barony - to Giacomo Barozzi. The Orthodox bishop was expelled and a Latin installed in his place. Santorini now became one of the four Latin bishoprics of the Duchy, and the fortress of Skaros was its capital. The Barozzi family governed Santorini until 1335, when it was returned to the Duchy of Naxos. From 1397 to 1418, Duke Giacomo Crispi governed the island. In 1480, Duke Giacomo III of Naxos gave it as dowry to Duke Domenico Pisani of Crete, but when Giacomo died his brother Giovanni III siezed it and so the island became part of the Duchy of Naxos again. In 1487, Santorini and all the other islands of the Duchy came under Venetian jurisdiction.

During their occupation of parts of Greece and afterwards, it was the policy of these Italian princes to strengthen their position by sending Jesuit missionaries to the islands and by encouraging the conversion of as many inhabitants as possible to the Catholic faith. At the same time, the Orthodox community was endeavouring to keep its language and faith alive through the founding of schools and churches.

Under the Latins, Santorini and the rest of the islands fell victim to rivalry among local princelings and to repeated looting by pirates, who had been plundering the coastline of the Aegean even in Byzantine times. For defensive purposes, therefore, five fortified towns (*castelia*) were built in the interior of the island: Skaros, the most important; Epanomeria (Epano Meria - Oia); Pyrgos, erected during the Byzantine era; Nimborio, and Akrotiri.

In 1537, Khair-ed-Din Barbarossa captured Santorini in the name of the Sultan. With the ousting of the Latins, the Orthodox Bishopric of Santorini was reinstated. Nevertheless, the island continued to be governed, even if in name only, by the Crispi dynasty until 1566. After the Crispis were finally supplanted, Santorini was ceded by the Sublime Porte to Joseph Nazis, who governed it for a short time until it was subjugated by the Turks in 1579. The Turks did not settle on the island. They merely renamed it Deyit-mejik - that is, 'little mill' - because of the many windmills there. During the Turkish occupation, the islanders enjoyed relative autonomy. In exchange for this privilege, they were obliged to pay tax both to the Sultan and to La Serenissma, the Republic of Venice. The Orthodox Bishopric was elevated to an Archbishopric. The system of law applied on the island was called the Civil Code of Santorini, and it seems to have been derived from Byzantine law. It was governed by Elders who were elected by the inhabitants and who in turn represented them before the Ottoman authorities. Every

*p. 35*

*The castle of Skaros, the most important of the five fortified settlements on Santorini during the Middle Ages.*

other year the Cadi, or Turkish judge, came to the island to dispense justice. During this period, piracy died down, making it possible for shipping to develop. Santorini gradually acquired a notable fleet of its own. The transit trade grew, too, making it easier to export local products, such as the celebrated wine of Santorini and cotton. Santorini inaugurated relations with all the major ports in the

Eastern Mediterranean. One indication of the prosperity that reigned during those days is the fact that in 1780 the monastery of the Prophet Elijah possessed its own ship. There were two shipbuilding yards, at Armeni in the Epanomeria district and at Athinios, and impressive mansions, which can still be seen today, went up in the villages. In the meantime, by the end of the 17th century, the class composed of descendants of the Latin conquerors had begun to decline, and as a result there was a considerable drop in the number of Catholics on the island. Shipping and trade continued to flourish into the early 19th century. In 1821, when the Greek War of Independence broke out, Santorini's fleet was the third largest in the country, after those of Hydra and Spetses.

However, the introduction of steam in the late 19th century brought an end to Santorini's shipping wealth, and the island's decline was tragically capped by the catastrophic earthquakes of 1956. Life was shattered. Most of the buildings were damaged, many collapsed completely. The event marked the start of the island's decay and abandonment, which continued into the 1970s. During this period, however, the interest of scientists, archaeologists, historians and geologists in Santorini's past began to shift it back to centre stage. As time went by, more and more people discovered the island. Reconstruction began, along with modernisation of Santorini's facilities. Today the past seems very distant. In summer, what was once among the neglected islands of the Aegean is like a buzzing beehive. For thousands of Greeks and foreigners it has become a favourite place to spend the whole summer, and for others it is an ideal holiday spot.

*p. 37*
*The church of Our Lady 'Episkopi' near the village of Mesa Gonia, built by the Emperor Alexius I Comnenus in the eleventh century.*

# Akrotiri - The prehistoric town

p. 38

A jug with breast-like protruberances from the Akrotiri site, ornamented with a scene showing swallows (Athens, National Archaeological Museum).

p. 39

The east side of complex D at Akrotiri.

Akrotiri is the best-preserved of all the prehistoric settlements discovered in the Aegean. Excavation of the site confirmed that the volcano had indeed erupted around 1500 BC, since the remains of the town were buried beneath a deep layer of volcanic ash.

Archaeologists began to investigate Akrotiri in the 19th century. In 1870, the French archaeologists H. Gorceix and H. Mamet, members of the French Archaeological School, on the instigation of their geologist compatriot, Fouqué, who had worked on the eruptions of the Santorini volcano, began excavations in the mine on Therasia and then turned their attention the area of Akrotiri on Thera itself. Later, the efforts of the French team were continued by the German baron Hiller von Gaertringen, who while conducting excavations at Mesa Vouno in search of Ancient Thera also began digging around Akrotiri.

In 1932, Spyridon Marinatos was struck - while digging at Amnissos in Crete - by the violence with which a Minoan villa had been destroyed and by the finding of pumice on another site close to the coast of Crete. These finds led him to

speculate that the collapse of Minoan civilisation might have been the result of the eruption of the volcano on Thera. He first published his theories in learned journals in 1939, and in 1967 he undertook to excavate at Akrotiri in the hope of finding evidence to confirm his beliefs. Professor Marinatos explored the site until his death in 1974, after which his work was continued by the archaeologist Christos Doumas, who has now uncovered a sizeable part of the town.

The prehistoric town of Akrotiri was the centre of a highly advanced civilisation which reached its zenith in about 1550-1500 BC (the period known as Late Minoan IA). The area had been continuously inhabited since the Neolithic period until a tremendous volcanic eruption laid a shroud of pumice and ash over everything that the islanders had so painstakingly created. Although Late Minoan Akrotiri was significantly influenced by Crete, which was then also at the height of its powers, it had also retained an identity of its own. The luxury and the quality of the houses revealed to date testify to the prosperity of

*p. 41*

*The Akrotiri site yielded a large number of jars which often contained remnants of the produce stored in them. On the left of the picture we can see a staircase leading to the upper floor of complex D.*

the settlement. Life in Akrotiri was comfortable and refined, just as it was for the Minoans of Crete.

The architecture of the city is strongly Cycladic. The houses were two - or three - storeys high with many rooms. The most luxurious were constructed of dressed stone (which is why the archaeologists call them 'xestes', meaning 'scraped'); the others were made of mud mixed with straw. The ground floor communicated with the upper floors by a

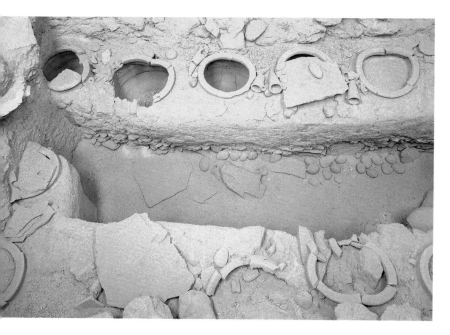

*p. 42*

*A row of jars built into a kind of counter on the ground floor of room 1 in complex D.*

wooden or stone interior staircase. To reinforce the buildings against earthquake tremors - which of course were particularly common in the area - wooden beams were used, as they were in Crete. The floors of the houses were usually of beaten earth. However, slabs of slate in regular shapes were also used, most commonly in the antechambers and in the rooms on the upper storeys. Elsewhere, the earth was inlaid with pieces of seashell (as in room A2 and on the first floor of B6), or covered with a kind of pebble mosaic (as in room D8). The roofs must have been flat and covered with a layer of earth for insulation, a technique common in the Cyclades until only a few years ago.

The storerooms, workshops and grain mills were always located on the ground floor. If a space

was used for food storage it had small windows to offer better preservation conditions. If it contained a workshop, mill or shop, then the room would have a large window placed right next to the door.

The rooms on the upper floors were where the family lived. Many of the walls were embellished with exquisite frescos. According to Professor Marinatos, the rooms with frescos were special places reserved for worship. On the upper floor(s) the windows were large and the rooms filled with light. The streets of the town were narrow and paved with flagstones. The drainage network consisted of stone-built sewers laid under the surface of the pavement. The sewage was led into these drains along clay pipes incorporated into the walls of the houses.

*p. 43*

*The ground floor of a house at Akrotiri. Wooden beams were inserid in the holes in the walls as a way of protecting the structure against earthquakes.*

# GUIDE TO THE ARCHAEOLOGICAL SITE AT AKROTIRI

The excavations conducted at Akrotiri to date have laid bare only part of the prehistoric town, which seems to have extended much further both to the east and to the west than is obvious today.

The modern visitor enters the site from the south and soon reaches the only street of the Akrotiri town to have been excavated. Along it as it runs from north to south through the town stand imposing groups of buildings, and the archaeologists have named it the **Street of the Telchines**: the Telchines were mythical demons (fire spirits) who were capable of destroying the earth with a special sulphurous liquid (cf. lava), but were also outstanding workers of metal.

The first building to the left of the entrance is **Xesti 3**, an impressive structure with at least three storeys and fourteen rooms on each floor. The street side of the building was faced with hewn stone. A staircase led up to the first floor, where many of the rooms were adorned with frescos such as that showing women picking crocuses. In the north-east corner was a 'purification basin', the only one of its kind found at Akrotiri. These were characteristic features of Minoan architecture, found in all the palaces on Crete. They were underground areas where those engaged in rites of purification or initiation were sprinkled with water. In the south part of the building many scattered stone tools were found. If we accept the theory that after the earthquake teams of workmen remained behind on the island to repair the damaged buildings, then it is possible that these tools belonged to them.

*p 45*

*Ground plan of the archaeological site at Akrotiri.*

N

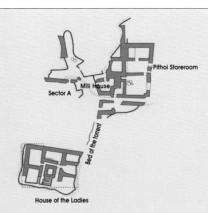

Pithoi Storeroom

Sector A

Mill House

Bed of the torrent

House of the Ladies

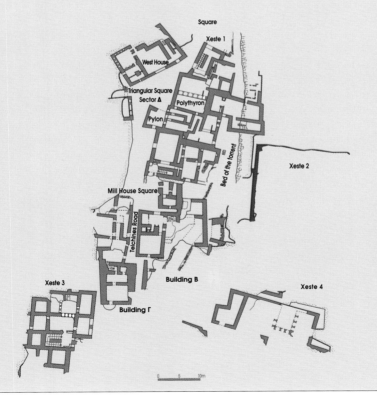

Square

Xeste 1

West House

Triangular Square

Sector Δ

Polythyron

Pylon

Bed of the torrent

Xeste 2

Mill House Square

Telchines Road

Xeste 3

Building B

Building Γ

Xeste 4

0    5    10m

As we step on to the Street of the Telchines and follow it to the north, the first building we see on our left is **building C**. Its entrance is right on the Street of the Telchines. Many stone tools were found here, too, and some of them were notably large. Directly opposite building C is the two-storey **building B**. On the ground floor, in room B1, a series of large storage jars were found, resting in special niches. Next to them were scattered cone-shaped funnels used for emptying the liquids. In room B2, on the same floor, there were numerous cooking vessels and some cone-shaped cups. The walls of the room above B1 were decorated with the frescos of the Boy Boxers and the Antelopes. while the Blue Monkey fresco was found in the room above B6.

Further along the road is the **Mill square**. It is bordered to the south and east by building B and on the north by **complex D,** and takes its name from the flour mill that was found in room D15, directly opposite room B1. The mill itself and the jar in which the ground flour was collected can still be seen. Complex D has four entrances. One of them, the western one, was protected by a porch. Room D2, in the east wing of complex D, was decorated with the Lily or Spring fresco. Traces of a bed and a footstool were discovered in the same room; a reconstruction of the bed is to be seen in the Archaeological Museum in Athens.

Passing through the gate, we find ourselves in **the Triangular square**. It is larger than the previous square and is bordered on the east and south by complex D, on the west by another building and on the north by the so-called West House.

The **West House** gives us a very clear picture of what the houses of Akrotiri must have looked like.

It is a two-storey structure, entered from the Triangular square. On the ground floor are storerooms and work areas, while the upstairs rooms are richly decorated with frescos. Room 4 contained a fresco showing a priestess, and in Room 5 the walls were adorned with frescos of two fishermen, a sea-battle, a riverside landscape and a convoy of merchant ships. The maritime subject-matter of these frescos led Professor Marinatos to surmise that the West House may have belonged to the chief admiral of the island's fleet. Room 4 also yielded a lavatory consisting of a clay seat with an opening from which a pipe ran into the main drain down the Street of the Telchines.

As we leave West House, we can see that the Street of the Telchines, beyond the north entrance to complex D, has been destroyed by the water from a torrent. We continue walking northwards. Now the Street of the Telchines is bordered on the west by the **house of the Women**, to our left. It was in the north wing of this building that the frescos of the Women and the Papyruses were found. It also yielded pottery, stone utensils and tools, among which was a half-finished marble object, most probably a vase.

Our itinerary has now led us to **section A**, the point where the excavation began in 1967. Three rooms in the northernmost part of section must have been storerooms, for many jars were found here. Some of them still contained carbonised flour

*p. 47*

*A marble vase (chalice) from Akrotiri. The absence of marble on Santorini means that this marvellous piece of workmanship must have been imported from one of the other islands in the Cyclades (Athens, National Archaeological Museum).*

and barley. There are large windows in the walls of these rooms, through which the stored goods were most probably distributed. The fragmentary fresco of the African was found in a room in this building.

## THE ECONOMIC AND SOCIAL ORGANISATION OF AKROTIRI

No written documents of any kind have been found in the prehistoric city of Akrotiri. This has meant that, in order to form any picture of the economic and social life there before the catastrophe, scientists have had to rely solely on the rich finds unearthed by the digs. Before discussing the theories on the social organization of Late Minoan Thera that have been formulated over time, let us look first at its economy.

The most important sectors of the island's economy were farming, pastoralism, fishing and shipping. Our evidence for this is the discovery of ancient jars filled with barley seeds, flour, and pulses such as yellow peas and other legumes. The islanders also must have cultivated sesame seeds and practised beekeeping, and were surely familiar with the olive, since so many amphorae - which were used primarily for transporting olive oil - have come to light. Bunches of grapes are often depicted on vases, revealing that vines were cultivated, too. This is borne out by the discovery of various jars which were used to store liquids. The Akrotirians also harvested crocuses, which yielded saffron for the dyeing of cloth. They raised sheep, goats and pigs and kept oxen as beasts of burden.

Apart from being farmers and herdsmen, they

were also fishermen. This has been deduced from the frescos, such as the one of the Fisherman, and from the fragments of fishbones and seashells found amongst the ruins and in amphorae.

The reputation of the Cycladic islanders as seafarers and scenes in frescos such as that showing the fleet lead to the conclusion that the citizens of Akrotiri must have had a well developed merchant navy. This would have permitted them to maintain trade with Crete and mainland Greece. The depiction in their frescos of subjects that are not native to Greece but rather related to the landscape of Egypt indicates that they also had contact with that region.

Furthermore, the discovery of a Syrian amphora shows that Akrotiri must have had some dealings with the peoples of the Eastern Mediterranean, as well.

The presence of looms in many of the houses demonstrates that the women were often occupied with weaving. Moreover, the large number of vases and other types of pottery tells us that another flourishing sector of the economy was that of ceramic production. The finding of stone tools and vessels, such as mills, pestles, hammers and the like, implies the development of masonry. Finally, the quality of the town planning, architecture and painting at Akrotiri shows that the Santorinians of that period were superb builders, engineers, masons and artists.

The architecture and the layout of

the settlement at Akrotiri reveal a good deal about the structure of its society. The kinds of room that existed in each building and their location (with the workshops and storerooms on the ground floor and the living quarters upstairs) lead us to the conclusion that each house lent a certain degree of self-sufficiency to its occupants. In addition, the fact that up to now more than one large, comfortable house has been excavated shows that the wealth of the area must have been fairly evenly distributed. Furthermore, no palace has yet been found, and therefore there may not have been a king. These observations have given rise to the theory that Akrotiri society was governed by the priestly class, which also controlled the economy.

The absence of any temples convinced Profes-

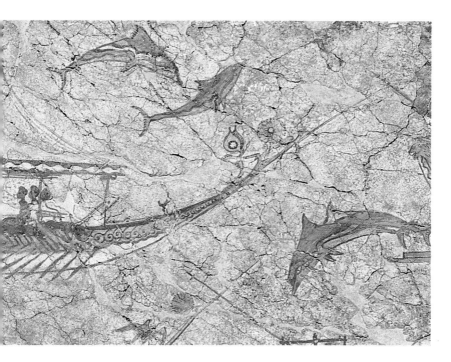

sor Marinatos that each house must have contained its own private place of worship. He formulated the idea that the Akrotirians must have worshipped nature and fertility, as was the case in neighbouring Crete. He maintained that the large free-standing buildings must have been the residences of important officials and that Xeste 3 was the religious and administrative centre of the community.

What, however, was the relationship between Late Minoan Thera and Crete? From all that we have already said, it is obvious that Akrotiri was self-sufficient economically. Although it was influenced by Minoan Crete in terms of architecture and the arts, its culture was largely its own. Consequently, Akrotiri cannot be thought of as a Minoan colony. In fact, Cretans must have taken up resi-

*pp. 50-51*

*Part of the Fleet or Convoy mural which adorned room 5 in the West House, showing one of the ships of Thera with its crew.*

*p. 52*

*A jug with breast-like protruberances painted with ears of barley*

*p. 53*

*A jug ornamented with bird motifs, one of the most superb examples of pottery from Akrotiri*

dence here to exploit the economic potential of the island and its inhabitants. In other words, it was a kind of trading station for Crete.

# POTTERY

Vast quantities of pottery have been found at Akrotiri: literally thousands of vessels, of which many have survived intact, standing upright in storerooms or on shelves and ledges. The pottery of Akrotiri falls into two categories: items which were made on the island, and those imported from other areas, such as the Argolid and especially Crete. A total of fifty different kinds of vessel have been found. The imported vessels were of excellent quality and bore ornamentation characteristic of their place of origin. Most of them were relatively small, thus making it easy to transport them. The local ware, by way of contrast, was highly varied in size and made from a kind of off-white clay. Against this background, abstract motifs or themes from the plant and animal worlds were painted in dark colours. Yet even the plant motifs of the local pottery were influenced by the corresponding Minoan themes which were in fashion in Crete at the time.

The vessels made by local crafts-

*p. 54*

*Above: a jug ornamented with spiral motifs (Athens, National Archaeological Museum).*

*Below: A wine-strainer, one of the most characteristic types of pottery found at Akrotiri, ornamented with spirals and plant motifs*

*p. 55*

*These cymbes, elongated vessels whose purpose remains unknown to us, are typical of the pottery of Thera*

men from Thera fall into two broad categories: those intended for everyday use, and luxury items. The luxury vessels are usually small, and much care and attention was evidently spent on making and decorating them. Among the most typical examples of Akrotiri ware are the special jugs called *prochoi*, which very often have a beak-shaped spout or two rounded protuberances on the neck. A theory has been advanced that these were used as ritual vessels for the pouring of libations during fertility rites. Of particular interest is their decoration with birds or plant motifs. Also typical of the local ware is the so-called *cymbe*, an elongated vessel whose use is unknown, and the *ethmus*, a kind of sieve with a perforated bottom.

The categories of Akrotiri ware include drinking-cups (which might be conical or shaped like lion's heads, tritons, etc.) for special use during rituals, sacrificial tables, round-bellied jugs, pans for carrying hot coals, and many others. Among the examples of Myce-

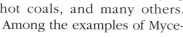

nean ware are amphorae with false mouths and the vessels known as *Keftiou* cups.

# PAINTING

The art that was most highly developed at prehistoric Akrotiri was painting. This is immediately evident in the many marvellous frescos that have been discovered so far. These frescos are not only genuine masterpieces in themselves: they also constitute invaluable sources for scholars seeking information on how people lived in that period.

The frescos of Thera are reminiscent of those at Cnossus in terms both of the techniques used and of the subject-matter. However, they have an artistic identity of their own. The technique is truly that of the genuine *buon fresco,* but the artist from Thera started to paint when the surface was still damp. As it dried, he continued working and by the time he finished, the surface

*pp. 56-57*

*Part of the Antelope mural from room 1 in complex B (Athens, National Archaeological Museum).*

was completely dry (*fresco secco*). The mineral
paints he used included the colours ochre, azure,
white, black, yellow and red.

The size of the surfaces covered by wall paintings varied, from small bands to large expanses of
wall or the pilasters of doors and windows. The
subjects portrayed, many of which are of a religious character, also displayed great variety: land-

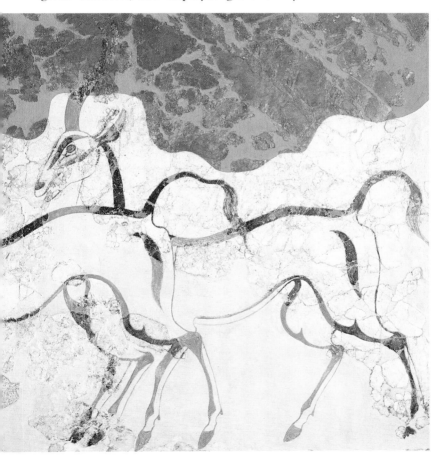

scapes and scenes inspired by nature, scenes with people, compositions depicting some real event, such as the miniature showing the fleet, and, finally, purely decorative motifs, such as rosettes and rhomboid shapes.

A characteristic feature of the Thera wall-paintings, apart from their vivid naturalism, is the freedom with which the subjects have been conceived and with which the artist expresses himself. The works show such fidelity and freedom of movement that they come very close to being real portraits. This leads one to the conclusion that the painter was not creating solely from his own imagination but that the subjects he was reproducing were familiar to him.

Today, thousands of years later, the beauty of the Akrotiri frescos continues to move us and has lost none of its power. They are on show in the Archaeological Museum in Athens and in the new Archaeological Museum at Fira. The most important of the frescos are as follows:

- The composition with the **Crocus Gatherers** from Xeste 3. This impressive fresco was spread across a number of walls in rooms on the ground floor and upper storey of the house, and shows women with lavish dress and ornaments picking crocus flowers. They are all turning in the direction of a seated female deity, who is protected by a winged griffin and accepts the gifts brought by the crocus gatherers, one of whom puts the flowers in a basket, from which a blue monkey takes them to give to the goddess.

- The fresco of **the Antelopes** from room 1 of complex B, depicting a pair of antelopes facing each other framed by a sprig of ivy. They are of the *Oryx beissa* species found in East Africa and are a

*p. 58*

*Part of the Blue Monkey mural from room 6 in complex B (Athens, National Archaeological Museum).*

*p. 60* ►

*The Boy Boxer mural from room 1 in complex B (Athens, National Archaeological Museum).*

*p. 61* ►

*One of the two fishermen who ornament corners of room 5 in the West House (Athens, National Archaeological Museum).*

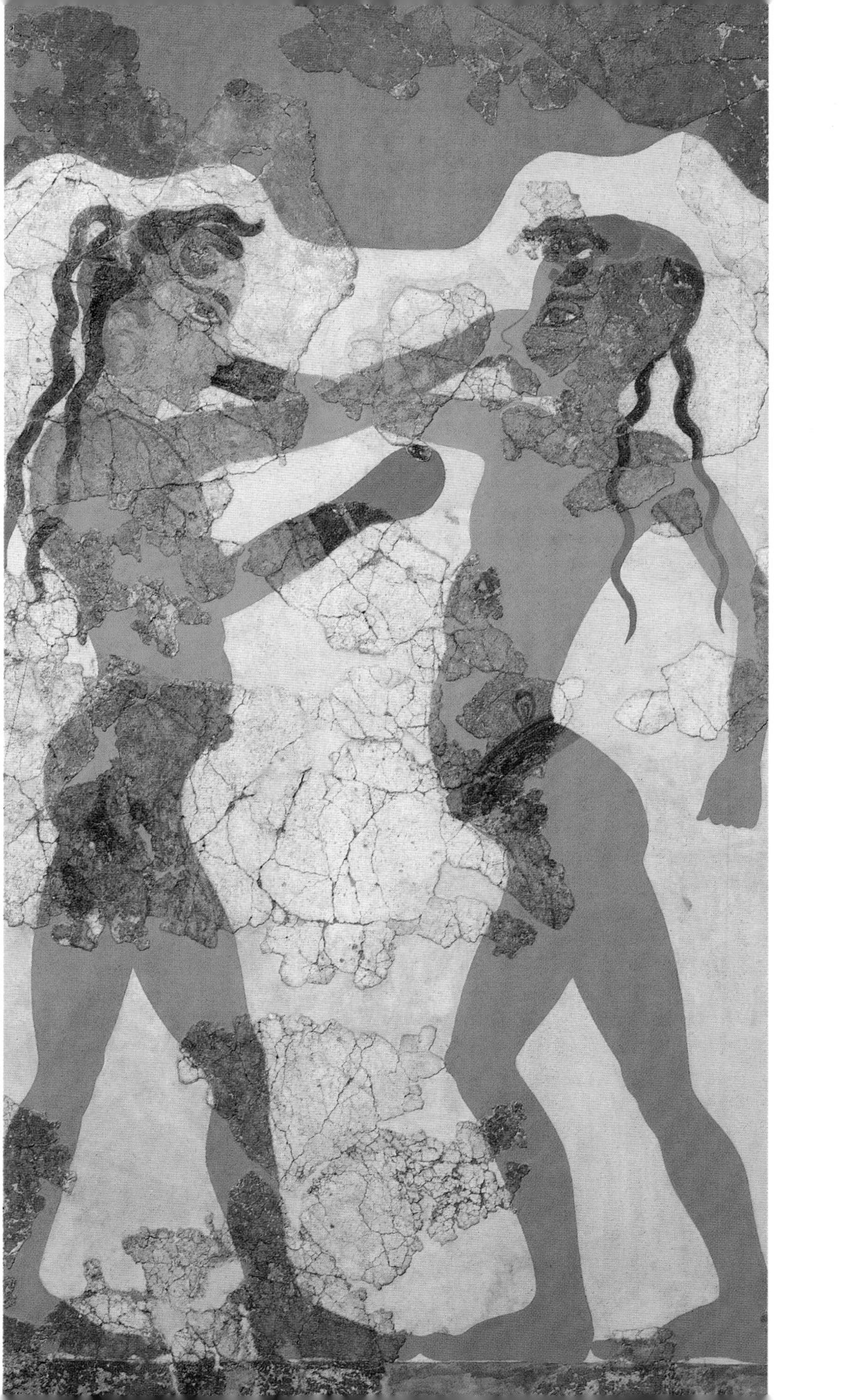

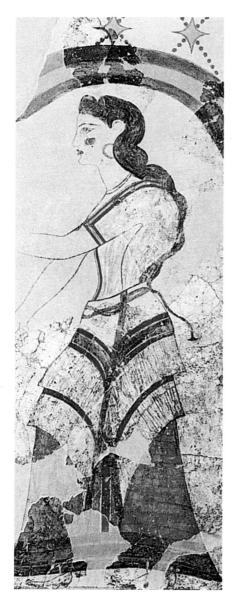

popular subject in Egyptian art of all periods. Here the figures of the animals have been rendered with simple, black outlines without recourse to many interior lines, the only exception being the heads, where certain details are shown in red. The result is most striking: the artist has succeeded, using the simplest of means, in giving his subject incredible precision and vitality.

- The fresco of the **boys boxing** from the south wall of the same room. The boys, each of whom wears a boxing glove on his right hand, are concentrating hard on avoiding one another's blows. The composition skilfully conjures up the intensity of the scene and the effort of the small pugilists. On their heads they must have worn blue wigs, under which their own long black curly locks can be seen. The boy on the left of the fresco is wearing more jewelry than his opponent: a blue necklace, bracelets and an earring.

- The fresco of the **blue monkeys** from room 6 of the same complex, depicting lively monkeys climbing up some rocks, evidently because they are being chased. The last one, who must be the leader of the band, is turning his head towards the pursuers. This wall-painting, too, although only a fragment survives, is full of vitality and movement.

- The fresco of **Spring** from room 2 of complex D. This is the only wall-painting in the Aegean that has been found intact. It

p. 62

*Part of the mural of the Women from the House of the Women (Athens, National Archaeological Museum).*

p. 63

*The Priestess mural from room 4 in the West House (Athens, National Archaeological Museum).*

*pp. 64-65*

*Part of the impressive mural of the Fleet or Convoy which covered a frieze
in room 5 of the West House (Athens, National Archaeological Museum).*

covered three of the four walls in the room. It portrays a rocky landscape with red lilies. The rocks, some yellow, others green or red, are curiously shaped, like those seen in volcanic areas. From amongst them triple lilies protrude, looking as though they are blowing in the Aegean breeze. These triple lilies are also found in wall-paintings in Crete, but there they are depicted with strict symmetry. Here, above the lilies swallows dart, as if in some courtship ritual. The presence of the swallows indicates that the season is spring. For scholars, geologists and volcano experts, this fresco holds enormous interest for it gives an unexpected glimpse of what Santorini looked like before the eruption.

- The fresco of the **Young Priestess** from room 4 in the fresco-covered West House. The woman appears to be holding an censer with lit charcoal and is wearing a heavy, perhaps woollen, robe.

- The frescos of the **Fishermen**, covering two corners of room 5 in the West House. They are each over 1 metre high. The men proudly show off their catch, the fish tied through the gills with a string.

- The miniature of **the Fleet** or **the Parade of Ships**. This fresco is of considerable historical interest, because it is a rich source of information about life in the Aegean in the mid or late 16th century BC. It covered the frieze above the windows of the south wall of the same room. This painting portrays the arrival and departure, amid celebrations, of a fleet sailing from from one harbour on the left side to another on the right. One of the ships must have been the flagship. The many flags and the presence of the residents,

*p. 67*
*The mural of the Papyrus from room 1 in the House of the Women (Athens, National Archaeological Museum).*

*pp. 68 - 69*
*Part of the River mural showing a semi-tropical landscape in room 5 of the West House. The wild vegetation and exotic animals are striking, but archaeologists still do not know whether they were native to Santorini or inspired by the tropics (Athens, National Archaeological Museum).*

some of whom seem to be waving goodbye while others wave in greeting, intensifies the festive atmosphere of the scene. The helmets strung from the masts of the sailing ships show that the passengers are warriors. The houses in the painting are multi-storeyed, constructed of dressed masonry and arranged on different levels - in fact, just like those that have been unearthed at Akrotiri. Apart from the architectural evidence it contains, the fresco is a mine of information about the animals and plants in the area, the clothes people wore, shipbuilding techniques and the way the various parts of the ship functioned in prehistoric times. The scene depicted in this painting most probably refers to a specific historical event.

- The miniature of **the River** or **Semitropical**

**Landscape**. This covered the band that divided the eastern wall of the above-mentioned room. A scene with figures of heroes, wild animals and birds is taking place by the river.

The north wall of the same room had a miniature which was executed on three levels: the first portrayed a **sea-battle**, the second some warriors holding long spears and wearing shields and helmets, and the third a pastoral scene.

- Five frescos showing **sea-going ships** from the West House.

- The fresco of the **Women** from room 1 of the House of the Women. The figures are dignified, with rouged cheeks and jewellery.

- Finally, the fresco of the **Papyruses** from the same room in the House of the Women.

*pp. 70 - 71*  ➤

*The famous Spring mural from room 2 of Complex D. The rocky outcrops with their blossoming lilies were probably typical of the landscape of the island before the earthquake. The swallows swooping above, alone or in pairs, are of the greatest beauty (Athens, National Archaeological Museum).*

# Ancient Thera

The second important period in the history of Santorini is linked with the city of Ancient Thera. The excavations there, begun in 1896 by Baron Hiller von Gaertringen in the area of Mesa Vouno, revealed ruins of a town which bore evidence of settlement as early as the 9th century BC. The mountain of Profitis Ilias, Santorini's highest peak, runs eastward into the lower rocky outcropping of Mesa Vouno. These two mountains are joined by a ridge named Sellada. Mesa Vouno, with an altitude of 369 metres, extends from west to south and its steep slopes plunge to the coast at Kamari to the north side and Perissa to the south.

This naturally fortified spot was an ideal place for the Spartan colonists to found their city, and they built two roads, one to the beach at Kamari, where they had their port (ancient Oia), and the other to Perissa. The strategic location of the town was appreciated later by the Ptolemies. In the 4th century BC, the most important era in the history of the island, Ancient Thera was transformed into an Egyptian naval base with the installation there of a large garrison.

Excavations in the area have brought to light a

*p. 73*

*The theatre of Ancient Thera, built under the Ptolemies in the third century BC.*

Hellenistic settlement that stretched from northwest to southeast. It was about 800 metres long
and its greatest width was 150 metres. It was split
in two by a central street, from which many side-
streets branched off. Because of the sloping terrain,
many of the alleyways were stepped. All the streets
were paved with flagstones, while the drainage
system consisted of a network of covered chan-
nels. Of the buildings that have been discovered,
the public ones were constructed of dressed limestone blocks, a material
found in abundance on
the island, while private
houses were made of
small stones of irregular
shape. The public build-
ings and the sanctuaries
lie to the right and left of
the main street. The pri-
vate houses are clustered
in two neighbourhoods,
one of which ascends the
west side of the moun-
tain, the other the east.

The excavations have
also brought to light two
cemeteries, one on the
southwest slope of Sella-
da, the other at the foot of
the cliffs of Mesa Vouno.
Both were in use during
the Geometric period and
down to the mid 7th cen-
tury BC. The cemetery
used in the 6th, 5th and

*pp. 74-75*

*The House of the
Phallus, in the
south Agora of
ancient Thera.*

4th centuries BC has been found on the northeast slope of Sellada. The older graves, as a rule, are to be found higher up than the later ones. Observing the same burial rites as the Dorians of Melos and Crete, the Therans used to cremate their dead. They would put the ashes in a special funerary urn made for the purpose and then place the urn along with libations inside the family tomb. In some cases, however, the corpse was simply buried without being cremated.

# GUIDE TO THE ARCHAEOLOGICAL SITE OF ANCIENT THERA

*p. 77*

*A Hellenistic female head of outstanding craftsmanship (Fira Archaeological Museum).*

The entrance to the archaeological site of Ancient Thera is from the northwest. We will be moving in a southeasterly direction. Within the site, apart from the buildings that belong to the Archaic, Hellenistic and Roman periods, we will be looking at the ruins of three churches. The first of these lies to the left of the entrance. This was an Early Christian basilica of the 4th/5th century, dedicated to the Archangel Michael. A Byzantine chapel of St Stephen was erected on the ruins of this basilica at a later date.

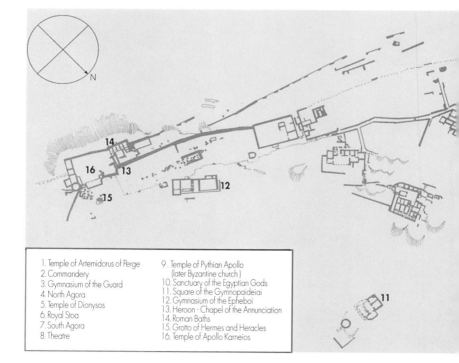

1. Temple of Artemidorus of Perge
2. Commandery
3. Gymnasium of the Guard
4. North Agora
5. Temple of Dionysos
6. Royal Stoa
7. South Agora
8. Theatre
9. Temple of Pythian Apollo (later Byzantine church)
10. Sanctuary of the Egyptian Gods
11. Square of the Gymnopaideiai
12. Gymnasium of the Epheboi
13. Heroon - Chapel of the Annunciation
14. Roman Baths
15. Grotto of Hermes and Heracles
16. Temple of Apollo Karneios

Our tour of the archaeological site begins with a visit to the **Temenos of Artemidorus of Perge**. Artemidorus, who came from Perge in Asia Minor, was the admiral of the fleet of the Ptolemies of Egypt. He founded the sanctuary at the end of the 4th or the start of the 3rd century BC. The temenos is carved out of the rock. Its facade bears the incised figures of a dolphin, an eagle and a lion, the symbols of Poseidon, Zeus and Apollo, respectively. The symbols of these gods, to the worship of whom the sanctuary was dedicated, are accompanied by inscriptions also incised in the rock. The sanctuary was also dedicated to the worship of oth-

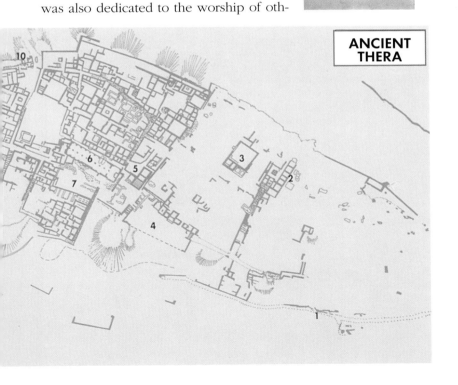

**ANCIENT THERA**

er gods, namely Concord, Priapus, Hecate, the
Cabeiri and the Heavenly Twins. Directly above
the symbol of Poseidon is inscribed the figure of
the sanctuary's founder, Artemidorus.

Continuing our tour, we come to a building on
our right which is called the **Stratonas or Gover-
nor's Palace.** It stands at the highest point in the
city, and a stepped road that starts at the main
street leads right to its main entrance. The Palace
consists of a series of rooms, which on three of the
four sides border on a square courtyard.

A short distance south of the Stratonas is what
has been named the **Gymnasium of the Guard**
because of its layout. This again has a large square
courtyard, on the east side of which are two rooms.

*p. 78*
*Part of the fa-
cade of the
Temenos of
Artemidorus,
with its reliefs of
a lion and an
eagle symbolising
Apollo and Zeus,
respectively.*

Following the main street, we come to a point where it becomes wider. We have reached the **Agora**, the most important public space in Ancient Thera (and any ancient city). It lies practically in the centre of the town and is divided by the main street into a north and south section. On the east side, and at a lower level, stretches one of the two residential neighbourhoods, while on the west there were temples and other public buildings. To the east there is an unrestricted view of the sea. The agora is 111 metres long, and its width varies from 17 to 30 metres.

Northwest of the North Agora, on our right, we come to three **Roman exedras** or platforms and immediately afterwards the small **Temple of**

*p. 79*

*Reliefs of a dolphin, symbolising Poseidon, and of Artemidorus of Perge, who founded the Temenos that bears his name in honour of Zeus, Poseidon and Apollo.*

**Dionysus,** where we climb up a broad stairway located on the side of the Agora. The temple dates from the Hellenistic period and consists of an antechamber (*pronaos*) and the temple proper (*cella*).

As we enter the South Agora, on our right we come to the so-called **House of the Phallus**, where there is a relief bearing the inscription "To my friends". Immediately beyond it is the **Basilike or Royal Stoa**, built in the 1st century AD, during the reign of the Emperor Augustus. It is 46 metres long and 10 metres wide, and has two entrances. The main entrance is on the long side, the other on the short one. Its north section was specially arranged to house statues of the imperial family. Its roof was supported by a central colonnade consisting of 10 Doric columns. At the point where the South Agora ends, the main street opens out again.

On our right we see the **Sanctuary of the Egyptian Gods**, Isis, Serapis and Anubis, hollowed out of the rock. To the southeast lies the **Temple of Pythian Apollo**, of which little remains because of the Byzantine church that was constructed on its foundations. On the left of the street is the **Theatre**, preserved today with alterations carried out by the Romans, though it was constructed in the 3rd century BC under the Ptolemies. Further south, behind the theatre, we come to the Roman **Baths**.

Further east is the chapel of the **Annunciation**. This was built upon a heroes' monument of the 2nd cen-

*p. 80*

*An Archaic statuette of a lion, from Thera (Fira Archaeological Museum).*

tury BC, which is nevertheless still in good condition. Such monuments were usually dedicated to the worship of the dead of the upper classes.

Continuing toward the southeast tip of the city, we come to the small Temple of **Ptolemy III the Benefactor**, then to the **Column of Artemis**, ultimately reaching the most important spot in Ancient Thera, the **Terrace of the Festivals**. This was where the extremely old Doric rite of the *Gymnopaediae*, dances by nude boys in honour of Apollo Karneios, took place. Celebrated in Dorian settlements throughout Greece, it was the primary festival for the Therans, and graffiti on the walls indicate that it was held as early as the 7th century BC. North of the Terrace of the Festivals stands the 6th century BC **Sanctuary of Apollo Karneios**. Its entrance, which is on the terrace, leads to a rectangular courtyard with a cistern for collecting rainwater. Southeast of the courtyard is the priest's residence. The temple, which opened to the northwest, is partly carved out of the rock and extends on to the terrace. It consists of a *pronaos* and *cella*, antechamber and temple proper.

South of the Terrace of the Festivals there is a small **cave** dedicated to the worship of **Hermes** and **Heracles.** Finally, at the southeast tip of town, we come to the **Gymnasium of the Ephebes**, a 2nd century BC building, and adjacent to it a later addition to the Roman Baths.

*p. 81*

*A relief of an eagle, symbolising Zeus, from the Temenos of Artemidorus at Ancient Thera.*

*p. 82*

*Terracotta female figurine, of the Daedalic period (seventh century BC). From the position of the hands, the figurine can be seen to portray a mourner.*

# THE ARTS

The earliest art form found in Ancient Thera is pottery from the Geometric period. Thanks to the burial customs just described, many works of pottery have survived in reasonably good condition.

Theran ceramics of that period and later, in the orientalising style, were influenced by neighbouring Naxos.

Nevertheless, the pottery from this time is perhaps the only work that can be attributed to Theran craftsmen. This is because from the 6th century BC and afterwards, the development of ceramics in other regions (Attica, Rhodes, Corinth, Ionia) and the location of Thera at a crossroads on the trade routes made it easy for the island to accept the wares of potters of other regions., and so local production stagnated.

Some Middle Geometric vessels (drinking cups with two horizontal handles) have survived. Among examples of Late Geometric work are jugs and amphorae used as funerary urns. The amphorae had to be rather large, because they held the offerings that accompanied the dead as well as the ashes. Such amphorae were the most characteristic

*p. 83*

*An Archaic storage jar with ornamentation in relief. At the neck of the vessel is a swan, and chariots with winged horses adorn the body of the jar (Fira Archaeological Museum).*

items made by Theran potters.

Apart from ceramics, examples of the plastic arts (sculptures) have also been found in Thera. Although it developed after pottery, perhaps because of the absence of the raw materials needed, such as marble, Thera has given us some of the most monumental works of Archaic sculpture that we know.

The two *kouroi* (statues of youths) dating from the second half of the 7th century BC, now in the

*pp. 84-85*
*Typical Theran vases of the Geometric period (Fira Archaeological Museum).*

Fira Archaeological Museum, and the *kouros* in the National Archaeological Museum in Athens, a work of the early 6th century BC known as the Apollo of Thera, are certainly among the best of their kind. All three must have originally stood over tombs in the ancient cemetery at Sellada. The two first must have been about 2 metres in height and were made of thick-grained island marble.

*p. 86*
*Hellenistic female figurine*

*p. 87* ➤
*Head of a large kouros, with the hair in the style familiar from other statues of the Daedalic period .*

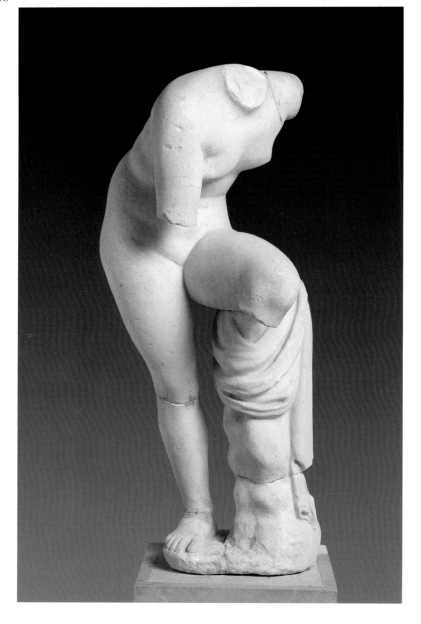

# Castles and Towers

*p. 88*

*The walls of the caldera in the vicinity of Skaros.*

*p. 89*

*Athinios bay; the promontory on which Skaros stands can be picked out in the background.*

During the Byzantine era and later, under Frankish occupation, the coasts of the Aegean suffered from incessant pirate raids. To protect themselves from this menace, islanders in particular built their settlements in inaccessible spots, or moved them there, and fortified them for even greater security. They also constructed watchtowers in high places, a kind of distant early warning system. In the Santorini of the 17th century, as we learn from the journals of the foreign travellers of the day, there were five such fortified settlements, the so-called *castelia*.

The most important, thanks largely to its position, was at Skaros, which was called simply 'The Castle'. 'Kastro' in Greek. Its 200 houses were perched on the summit of a steep, impregnable rocky promontory. To reach its walls a walk of at least half an hour was required. A large bell, which was hung at the top of the rock, warned the inhabitants of impending danger. Skaros was where the Latin lords, island officials and the Catholic archbishop resided; it was the medieval capital of Thera.

After 1700, when the pirate threat began to diminish, the Castle gradually fell into ruin. Its inhabitants founded a new settlement, Fira, at a lower point.

The castle of Epanomeria or Apano Meria stood in the vicinity of present-day Oia. It was also known as the castle of St Nicholas. The other three castles were situated in the south part of Santorini. Pyrgos ('Tower') or Kainouryiopyrgos ('New Tower') was erected during Byzantine times in the centre of the village by the same name, and the villagers could take shelter there in the event of enemy attack. It was here that the representative of the Ottoman authorities would stay on his bIannual visit to the island to administer

*p. 90*

*View of Oia with the castelli of Epanomeria or Apano Meria.*

justice. Pyrgos had about 100 houses and four churches, of St James, St John the Divine, the Holy Trinity and the 'Theotokaki' (the 'Little Virgin'). The castle of Nimborio or Emborio, with 80 houses, was where commercial transactions took place. Finally, there was the castle of Akrotiri or Poundas, (meaning 'on the cape'), with about 200 houses, of which only a few ruins remain today.

Apart from the fortified settlements or castles, Santorini also had a good many *goulades:* these were isolated towers for defensive purposes that stood either inside or outside the fortress walls. These were used as places for storage of foodstuffs

*p. 91*

*Panoramic view of Pyrgos, where one of the most important medieval castellia of Thera was located.*

or lodging for the feudal lords, as well as refuges in case of enemy attack. We know that there were such towers at Epanomeria (Oia), of which only the base has survived, at Nimboreio, which was built on the outskirts of the settlement and has been preserved almost intact, at Akrotiri, in the centre of the castle and, finally, at Fira.

The islanders who did not have access to sanctuary in the castles or *goulades* during enemy raids used to hide in the caves which abound on the island. There are caves at Vothonas (called 'Our Lady in the Hole'), Megalo Chorio, the Katefiani chapel at Perissa, and elsewhere.

The watchtowers were manned by sentinels who kept a sharp watch over their districts and warned the people when pirates appeared on the horizon.

*p. 92*

*The goulas of Nimborio or Emborio.*

*p. 93*

*The Theoskepasti chapel on the Skaros promontory.*

# Vernacular and Ecclesiastical Architecture

*p. 94*

*House roof, showing a chimney of the type often encountered on Santorini.*

*p. 95*

*View of Oia. Oia and Fira are the two most typical linear villages on the island.*

The singular topography of Santorini has contributed decisively to the evolution of its special indigenous architecture. Its characteristic architectural style, although belonging generally to the architecture of the Aegean, is notable for many individual features and forms of marked plasticity. This is because it has exploited to the full the unusual landscape and possibilities of the place.

The construction materials used by the local craftsman in building are exclusively volcanic in origin. They include black stone, red stone, ash and pozzolana (pumice).

Houses roofed with barrel or groin vaults and houses dug out of the vertical face of the lava cliffs: these are the principal building types on the island. The dugout structure illustrates the ingenuity of the locals in the search for easy, inexpensive housing. The vaulting is a consequence of the need to economise on wood, which is in very short supply on the island.

*p. 96*

*The landscape of Santorini would not be the same without its scores of tiny chapels, which blend harmoniously into the colours and lines of nature.*

In their present form, the settlements on Thera can be separated into those built on the rim of the cliff facing the caldera (the so-called linear settlements of Fira, Oia and Therasia); those that developed outside the walls of the castles in various directions (the expanded fortress villages of Pyrgos, Emborio and Akrotiri); and the dug-out or troglodyte neighbourhoods. These are the settlements whose original form followed the banks of a riverbed and eventually spilled over into a more fertile district, as at Finikia, Vothonas, Karterado.

In terms of construction methods, Santorini's

houses fall into three categories: troglodyte, semi-built and built. The troglodyte dwellings are those which have been completely hollowed out of the volcanic earth, the semi-built have some extra sections above ground, and the last are those which have been constructed in the usual manner.

The troglodyte houses, which belonged to the poorest of the islanders, were relatively long with a narrow frontage. This facade was always supplemented with a built wall, which closed off the living area. They had a vault-shaped roof, it too hollowed out of the lava. The resulting long, narrow space

p. 97

*View of Oia. Houses of all the island types - built, semi-built and underground (bottom left) - can be seen.*

*p. 98*

*A typical courtyard gate in Santorini.*

*p. 99*

*View of Oia. Note, in particular, the houses with vaulted roofs, one of the features of the island's architectural character.*

was divided by a built wall into two sections, with the living area in front and the bedroom, less well lit, in the back. Apart from the door, the built facade usually had three other symmetrical openings: a window on either side of the door and a kind of skylight shaped like a half-moon above the door. These apertures were repeated in the interior partition wall, bringing both light and air to the back room. The kitchen, with a fireplace for cooking, consisted of a low, built corner with a vaulted ceiling that was connected with the living area. The lavatory was located outside the house with access from the courtyard. The courtyard also usually contained a cistern, which was an indispensable part of every house, rain being the only source of water on Santorini, as on many of the other Cyclades.

In the semi-built houses, one side, generally that

of the entrance, is constructed, while the rest is underground. The roof over the built sections might be a barrel or cross vault or it could consist of stones mixed with pozzolana (pumice which can form a type of cement when pulverized and mixed with water) poured into a mould until it hardened.

In terms of type, the dwellings of Santorini fall into three categories: farm houses, ordinary people's town houses, and the mansions of the more affluent.

The farm house is situated outside the limits of town or village. It has a large courtyard and several auxiliary buildings (stable, chicken coop, outdoor oven, and inevitably a cistern or tank for collecting rain water). These houses may be either dug out or built, depending on their location. They usually have only one storey, but this also is a function of the surrounding topography. The oven, which is cylindrical in shape, is normally placed in the courtyard. An indispensable complement to the majority of the island's farm houses, particularly those in areas where vines are cultivated, is the wine press. The wine press with its characteristic arched double door and the barrels, or *voutsia* as the locals call them, had several rooms for pressing the grapes and other purposes. It was often lit by a hole in the middle of the roof, which could be closed from above with stones.

The town houses of ordinary people, standing in the centre of the villages where construction is dense, have limited space to work with. This is why they are frequently irregular in shape, consisting of many storeys, with auxiliary areas on different levels to the rooms in which the families lived. There is less room for animals than in the farm house. As for furniture, it was confined to the absolutely essential:

*p. 100*

*Above: the interior of a Santorini house.*

*Below: facade of a vaulted house, with the characteristic chimney.*

chests for clothes, linen, and food; tables, chairs, wooden sofas and sideboards - the items found all over the Aegean islands which became widely used with the growth of shipping. Since the poorer families slept on the floor, European-style beds must originally have been a luxury reserved to the rich.

The mansion house, like the dwellings of ordinary people, is to be found in the middle of the towns and villages. In its initial form it must have resembled its humbler counterpart, as both house types evolved from the dwellings constructed within the castle precincts. Their imposing size and symmetrical facades, which are their most obvious features today, must have been acquired later on.

*p. 102*
*Oia, view of the town.*

The monumental mansion houses are mainly a product of the 19th century, as can be seen from the dates inscribed above their doors. Their owners

generally belonged to the merchant class, as maritime trade was flourishing by that time. Their design must have been Italian in origin, based on Renaissance models. The facades of these houses are geometric, faced with dressed red stone. Their roofing consists of groin vaults and monastery-type domes, the so-called *skafes* (in the shape of an upturned boat), covered by a flat roof.

The mansion house was so popular in Santorini that the passion for the neo-Classical style, so prevalent in other parts of Greece, never caught on there.

There are some neighbourhoods in the settlements of Santorini that consist solely of mansion houses. The Sidera quarter of Oia is where the 19th century sea-captains built their homes. They stand on or near the gently-sloping or flat side of the town, where there is plenty of space among the houses;

*p. 103*
*Oia, part of the town.*

the dwellings of ordinary sailors are located much nearer the precipice, where the density is high and the houses dug out. At Messaria, too, the houses of the gentry stand in the central district.

On Santorini, apart from the private ovens in the farm houses, there were buildings in the various neighbourhoods that functioned exclusively as bakeries for the use of the community. They were usually joined to the home of the baker himself, though in a few instances they were adjuncts of a flourmill. More often, the mills were isolated structures situated outside residential areas. When the bakery and the mill functioned as a single unit, then the bakery and the main dwelling would be built on a different level from the mill, usually below ground, so as not to interfere with its operation. The mills of Santorini are the same as those found all over the Cyclades. They are cyclindrical with an articulated roof and arms with the sails, which turn in all winds and move the top millstone. The rubbing of the top millstone on the bottom one grinds the wheat and other grain into flour.

The churches of Santorini, although very much a part of the island's cubist architecture style, show a Western influence in their relatively large size. The volcanic eruptions and catastrophic earthquakes that have shattered the island from time to time strengthened the religious fervour of the locals, which intensified when they were confronted with Catholicism during the Frankish occupation. Thus, before the 1956 earthquake, the island boasted some 260 churches. Most of those that have survived are of the one-aisled domed basilica type, although there are also domed cruciform churches. The dome, which may be painted white - as are

*p. 104*

*One of the windmills which are a common sight on Santorini.*

pp. 106-107

*A characteristic example of the ecclesiastical architecture of Santorini.*

most of the churches - or blue, is frequently divided into segments and sometimes there is a lantern on top, a purely Renaissance touch. On the facades of the churches are twin bell towers, often big enough for cathedrals. Santorini's monasteries - such as that of the Prophet Elijah - are massive and often reminiscent of fortresses. They have an inner courtyard, arcades and impressive bell towers.

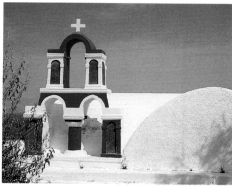

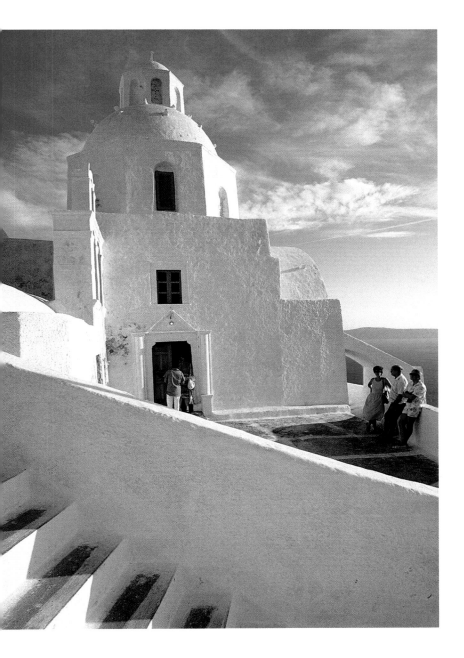

# THE SIGHTS

## *Fira*

Fira, also known as Chora, is the capital of Santorini. It has a permanent population of 1,718 residents (1990 census) and is built on the rim of the caldera some 260 metres above sea level. The volcano lies exactly opposite, still emitting puffs of steam. The spectacular architecture of its dazzling white houses, that seem to cling to the dark sides of the caldera, and the incomparable view of the volcano and the open sea combine to make Fira one of the most breathtakingly beautiful places in Greece.

*p. 109*
*The town of Fira, clinging to the brow of the towering cliffs above the caldera, seems to be hovering between earth and sky.*

The town dates from 1810, when the inhabitants of Skaros, no longer terrified by the pirate threat, began to abandon the castle and establish themselves in this lower flatter area, with access to the sea.

Fira is a long, narrow collection of buildings with steep, narrow, stepped alleyways. The houses on the caldera

side are dug-out dwellings, constructed on different levels, one above the other so that the roof of one forms the courtyard of the next.

The town can be reached by car or bus from Athinios, the port for Fira and the only harbour on the island where ships can dock. It can also be reached from Mesa Yialos, the spot usually chosen by the cruise liners. From there the ascent up the 500 or so steps to Fira may be made by funic-

*p. 112*

*A view of the centre of Fira, where the heart of life on the island beats.*

ular, on foot or on donkeyback.

Among its best preserved districts is Kato Fira. The churches of St Menas and of Christ are located here, both masterpieces of ecclesiastical architecture. The former has a typical SantorinIan dome, and the latter an exquisitely carved screen and bishop's throne.

On the border between the Catholic and Orthodox quarters stands the Archaeological Museum of

*p. 113*

*View of Fira. On the right, the church of St Menas.*

Fira. It houses the finds from the excavations at Akrotiri and Mesa Vouno, including:

- vases and figurines of the Early Cycladic period (2500-2000 B.C.)

- pottery from Akrotiri (1550-1500 B.C.)

- Geometric and Attic vases and figurines of the 8th and 7th centuries B.C.

- sculpture of the Archaic, Hellenistic and Roman periods.

A new museum (called 'the New Museum') was recently founded in Fira, and contains a collection of interesting wall-paintings from Akrotiri.

There are two Catholic convents in the Catholic quarter, belonging to the Sisters of Mercy, founded in 1841, and the Dominican nuns, where the Greek Handicrafts Organization has a school

*p. 114*

*Panoramic view of Fira.*

*p. 115*

*There are little churches all over Fira, giving the town a charm all its own.*

for carpet weaving.

Apart from the sights it has to offer, Fira is the centre of life on Santorini. There are numerous hotels, restaurants, bars, cafes and discos to satisfy the visitor, as well as shops selling everything from folk arts and crafts - pottery and hand-woven fabrics - to costly gold jewelry.

*pp. 116-117*
*Views of the town*
*of Fira.*

## *Firostefani*

Near Fira is Firostefani, another long, narrow settlement built along the rim of the caldera. Boasting a superb view of the volcano, it has a picturesque square, a church dedicated to St Gerasimos - the only church on the island to be surrounded by cypress trees - hotels and restaurants.

Between Firostefani and Imerovigli or Merovigli, which is the next settlement on the caldera rim, stands the old Orthodox monastery of St Nicholas. It was founded by the Ghizi family and was origi-

nally located at Skaros. In 1651, the monastery housed an order of nuns. It moved to its current position in 1890.

## Imerovigli

The name of this village belongs to the days of the pirates: *vigla* = watchtower, *imera* = day. Its position at the centre and highest point of the caldera rim gave it visual command of the whole area, enabling it to signal timely warnings to the population when pirates sailed into view. It also derived im-

*pp. 118-119*

*Firostefani offers visitors a superb view over the caldera and the volcano.*

p. 122
*View of Imerovigli, with the Orthodox monastery of St Nicholas.*

portance from its proximity to the fortress at Skaros. The 'Malteza' church has a marvelous carved wooden screen with icons depicting scenes from the Old Testament. There is a path from Imerovigli leading to Skaros.

# Skaros

p. 123
*The rocky peak and castle of Skaros. The Theoskepasti chapel can be picked out, bottom right.*

Up here you can see what remains of the old castle (see 'Castles and Towers'). The path, which heads south initIally and then bears west, ends at the white-washed chapel of the Our Lady 'Theoskepasti', which looks as though it has been hollowed out of the rock

# *Oia*

Sometimes referred to as Apano Meria, Oia is
linked by 10 kilometres of paved road to Fira and
faces Therasia. It is actually a collection of six villages: Oia, Perivolas, Finikia and Tholos on the
ridge and Ammoudi and Armeni at the base of the
caldera. Oia stands lower  than Fira, nearer the
sea, which is reached by two sets of cobbled steps.
The one to Ammoudi has 214 steps, the other to
Armeni has 286.  Down at Armeni, looking as
though it has been hollowed out of the rock,
stands the little church of St Nicholas, a short distance from the coast.

*pp. 126-127*

*Oia is one of the
most attractive
places on San-
torini.*

The existence of Oia is referred to well before
1650. Under the Franks, it was the capital of one of
the five administrative districts into which Santorini

*p. 128*

*View of Oia, with its churches and the carefully-tended courtyards of the houses.*

was divided. Oia reached the peak of its prosperity in the late 19th and early 20th century. Its economic development was based on its merchant fleet, which plied the Eastern Mediterranean and especially the route from Alexandria to Russia. In 1890, Oia boasted 2,500 inhabitants and 130 of the ships in Santorini's fleet, while there was a small shipyard

at Armeni. Today, Oia is Santorini's second-largest
village. It is less cosmopolitan than Fira, but in its
way it is more picturesque and is without doubt
one of the most beautiful places on the island. It
has a great many troglodyte houses, carved out of
the cliffside by the crews of the merchant ships for
their families. The two-storey captains' houses, built

*p. 129*

*Oia stands out for its incomparable view of the caldera and its unusual architecture.*

at the highest part of the village, are a reflection of its former affluence. The streets of Oia are paved with slabs of marble rather than the cobblestones encountered elsewhere on the island. There are churches of singular beauty, and the sunset at Oia is justly renowned.

Of the castle that once defended Oia, only a few stones remain; the same is true of the tower that stood on the highest spot in the vicinity. Inside the tumbled walls of the castle, on the edge of the cliff, there is a church dedicated to Our Lady of Platsani. Oia has a small museum of maritime history.

*pp. 130-131*
*Views of Oia.*

# Messaria

Messaria lies 3.5 kilometres south of Fira, in the interior of the island, amidst vineyards and vegetable gardens. Much of Santorini's wonderful wine is produced around the village. Messaria also has a number of hotels and restaurants to house and feed summer visitors.

# Vothonas

Picturesque Vothonas, built up the hillside like an amphitheatre to the east of Messaría, is almost an extension of its neighbour. In this farming village, which has 300 inhabitants, there is a church dedicated to St Anne, with a lovely carved screen whose icons depict scenes from the Old Testament.

# Exo Gonia

South of Vothonas is Exo Gonia, a small village that seems to climb up the mountainside. Worth a visit here is the church of St Charalambos. Built on a hill, Exo Gonia can seen from virtually every corner of the island.

*p. 135*

*Above: general view of the village of Mesaria.*

*Below: the village of Vothonas.*

# *Pyrgos*

Pyrgos, at the foot of Mt Profitis Ilias, is an example of a settlement that was fortified in the Middle Ages; it is the only village in Santorini where the medieval features and atmosphere have been so vividly preserved. Its streets, which follow the contours of the hillside, divided the village into zones. The walls of the outermost houses were an integral part of the village fortifications. When the danger of pirate raids diminished, the inhabitants started to build homes outside the walls, giving the village its present form.

*pp. 136-137*

*Pyrgos, at the foot of Mt Profitis Ilias, is one of the most traditional villages on Santorini, and the one where medieval features are most noticeable.*

There are many churches worth seeing in Pyrgos. The oldest, known as the Theotaki, is dedicated to the Dormition of the Virgin. It was erected in the 11th century a little after the church at Episkopi Gonia. Between 1537 and 1650, other churches were built: the Transfiguration of Our Lord, St Theodosia and the 'dug-out' church of St Nicholas 'Kissiras'. The church of the Presentation of the Virgin, with its carved screen, dates from between 1650 and 1664. Later churches include those of St Catherine (1660), St George (1680), the Archangel Michael (1690) and St Nicholas (1700). Near Pyrgos, crowning Mt Profitis Ilias, is a monastery dedicated to the

Prophet Elijah. The solid facade of its exterior walls, perforated with just a few windows, is reminiscent of a fortress. It was founded in 1711 and built in two phases, 1711 to May 1724 and November 1852 to March 1857.

The monastery was subject to the Patriarchate of Constantinople. Until 1860 it was cenobitic, while until 1853 no women were permitted to enter it. In earlier times, the monastery of the Prophet Elijah possessed considerable wealth. It even had its own ship which conducted trade for

the benefit of the monastery. At the same time, it was also an active intellectual and patriotic influence. From 1806 to 1845 it ran a school where Greek language and literature were taught to children. The monastery's decline began in 1860. Its buildings suffered serious damage in the earthquakes of 1956.

Today the monastery has an important collection of ecclesilastical treasures, manuscripts and old and more recent books, as well as ethnographic materIal. The carved wooden screen in

*pp. 138-139*

*Panoramic view of Pyrgos. In the background, Fira and Oia.*

the main church is notable.

Near **Mesa Gonia**, a farming village with a wine production and storage plant, is the most important Byzantine monument on the island, the church of Our Lady 'Piskopi' or Episkopi Gonia. Founded by the emperor Alexius I Comnenus in the 11th century, it is dedicated to the Dormition of the Virgin. At some point in its history it may have been used as the main church of a monastery and it also served as the seat of the bishop of Santorini. It has undergone many alterations and additions, however, since the 11th century. The only thing that has remained intact from Byzantine times is its carved marble screen. The frescos have been dated to ca. 1100.

*p. 140*

*The pretty bay at Athinios is the port for Fira and the only safe harbour on the island.*

*p. 141*

*Above: general view of the village of Athinios.*

# *Athinios*

This picturesque cove, located about 11 kilometres from Fira, constitutes the island's only harbour. A few houses have sprung up around it, along with some tavernas. To the right of the quay is a pretty, small, pebbly beach.

*p. 141*

*Below: the red beach, one of the most striking on Santorini.*

## *Megalochori*

Situated to the south of Athinios, this inland village belies its name ('Big Village'), having only some 250 inhabitants.

*p. 142*
*A superbly-crafted belltower in the village of Emborio.*

## *Emborio*

The largest village in the south part of the island stands in the heart of a fertile plain. During the

VenetIan occupation, Emborio was one of Santori-ni's five castles as well as being its trading centre, as its name implies (Emborio = trade, commerce in Greek). On the mountain opposite, we can still see the windmills that also contributed to the prosperity of the district. The people of Emborio, called *Boryiani*, were also renowned seafarers. In former times a man with a lantern used to walk from house to house before dawn to wake up the fishermen - a kind of community alarm clock. The port for Emboreio was Perissa.

*p. 143*
*General view of Emborio. On the left, the goulas of Emborio.*

# *Perissa*

One of the most popular beaches on Santorini and one of the most geared to tourism, Perissa has coarse black sand. There are plenty of hotels, restaurants and other facilities. The east side of the beach is overshadowed by the dark hulk of Mesa Vouno. There are also two churches worth seeing, the Holy Cross and St Irene (late 16th-early 17th century).

*pp. 144-145*

*Perissa, the tiny harbour for Emborio, is the most popular and crowded beach on Santorini. Its sandy expanse stretches far along the coast.*

# *Kamari*

*pp. 146-147*

*Kamari was the
port of Ancient
Thera. Now it has
developed into a
tourist resort, and
the beach has a
full range of
amenities.*

This was the port for Ancient Thera and in those days it was called **Oia**. Today it is the second most popular beach on the island. The long beach with its fine black sand is protected to the south by the vertical mass of Mesa Vouno. Here, apart from clear water for swimming, there are hotels of all kinds, tavernas, restaurants, discos, a campsite, bars and a cinema.

# *The Volcano*

The crater of the volcano is on Nea Kammeni, the islet formed by the most recent eruptions of the volcano. It is a mass of black matter, which is simply lava that poured as a viscous liquid from the bowels of the earth and then hardened.

The caique which takes visitors there from Thera anchors off the coast of the little island, where the water is warm and made translucent green by the sulphur content. From the beach there is a path right up to the rim of the crater. The walk takes about half an hour. Near the crater, puffs of steam smelling strongly of sulphur are emitted from cracks at many points. Visitors intending to walk to the crater should wear stout shoes and take a good supply of drinking water.

*pp. 148-149  Views of the Volcano*

# Therasia

The area of this island is no more than 16 square kilometres (5.7 km. long, 2.7 km. at its broadest. This remnant of the west coast of prehistoric Strongyle is home to-day to some 250 people. Although it has the same geographical configuration as Santorini, Therasia has not experienced the same rapid tourist development.

The west coast of the island slopes gently into the sea, backed by a fertile valley where the inhabitants, farmers for the most part, grow grapes, split yellow peas, barley and tomatoes.

The east coast, in contrast, ends abruptly in steep cliffs. The island's biggest village, also called Therasia, is built on the rim of the precipice. Two hundred and seventy steps link it to the coast and the tiny harbour.

Therasia has same cobbled paths and the same architecture as the larger island, and its view of the caldera is just as spec-tacular. There are two other hamlets on Therasia, Potamos with 90 inhabitants and Agrilla, which is deserted. On the south coast of the island, near the sea, there is a cave called Trypiti (which means 'perforated'), while to the north stands the chapel dedicated to St Irene, which some scholars believe gave San-torini its name. (Other experts say that the name is from St Irene at Perissa.)

*p. 153*

*General view of Therasia.*

# Useful Information

## HOW TO GET THERE

### By ferryboat:

*Ferries leave Piraeus daily bound for Santorini (distance 130 nautical miles). The trip lasts about 12 hours. For information about ferry schedules from Piraeus to Santorini, call the Piraeus port authority,(210)451.1311.*

### By plane:

*Santorini is linked with Athens by daily Olympic Airways flights. For information, call Olympic Airways, Athens (210)966.6666. The flight takes about one hour. There are also direct flights between Mykonos, Herakleio, Rhodes and Santorini, while many charter flights connect the island with major European cities. Santorini airport is about 7 kilometres from Fira. Olympic Airways buses carry passengers to and from the airport.*

### Inter-island connections:

*Ferries connect Santorini regularly with the following islands: Ios, Naxos, Paros, Syros, Sikinos, Folegandros, Sifnos, Serifos, Kimolos, Melos, Mykonos, and Herakleio, Crete. For information. call the harbour master at Santorini (22860)22.239. You can also fly to Mykonos, Herakleio and Rhodes. For information, call the OA offices in Athens (210)966.6666 or at Santorini (22860)22.493.*

## STAYING ON THE ISLAND

### Accommodation:

*Accommodation is available in a wide range of hotels, pensions, guest houses, bungalows, furnished apartments and rented houses and rooms. These are divided into five categories and are to be found in all the large villages on Santorini. There are also two campsites, one at Kamari (capacity 570, 22860/31.451) and the other at Perissa (capacity 249, 22860/81.343).*

*For a stay in exceptionally pleasant, traditional surroundings, the GNTO has restored some old houses in Oia and converted them into pensions. Not only do they have a stupendous view of the caldera, they are also fully equipped for*

*self-catering. For information, call (22860)71.016, 71.234. For more information regarding hotel accommodation, get in touch with the Hotel Chamber of Greece, 24 Stadiou St., tel: (210)323.6962, telex: 214.269 XEPE GR, fax: (210)322.5449, postal address XENEPEL.*

*For on-the-spot reservations, the GNTO has a branch office at Karageorgi Servias and 2 Stadiou St on Syntagma Square in Athens (inside the National Bank of Greece), tel: (210)323.7193 from Monday to Friday, 08.00 - 14.00.*
*The Tourist Police on Santorini will also help you find a place to stay.*

### Getting around on the island

*There are buses between Fira and Imerovigli-Vourvoulo-Oia/ MessarIa-Pyrgos-Akrotiri/ MessarIa-Pyrgos-Megalohori-Emborio- Perissa/ Kamari/ Monolithos. There are also a number of taxis (22860/22.555) and several rent-a-car or rent-a-motorbike agencies. Organised excursions to the most important sites are offered by the island's travel agencies.*

*From Skala below Fira caiques depart for Therasia, PalIa and Nea Kammeni. Therasia can also be reached by caique from Oia.*

### Where to go for entertainment

*There are tavernas serving grilled meat, pizza restaurants, souvlaki shops and cafes offering ouzo and titbits with a stupendous view of the volcano all over the island. In the more frequented places, such as Oia, Perissa, Kamari and Emborio, there discos and bars to complement your nightlife, while at Emborio and Pyrgos there are nightclubs with live bouzouki music. Island delicacies worth tasting include fava (puréed split yellow peas served with a little oil, lemon and chopped onion), pseftokeftedes ('fake meat-balls' made of tomatoes, flour, onions, and herbs), chloro (a fresh, particularly delicious local cheese), and the famous Santorini wine.*
*Throughout the year there are paniyirIa, saints' days celebrated with abundant food and drink and folk music played on traditional instruments to accompany dancing. Among the most important of these are:*
*- The feast of the Prophet Elijah, 20 July, at Fira.*
*- The feasts of Our Lady, 15 August and the Transfiguration of Our Lord, 6 August, at Akrotiri.*
*- The feast of Our Lady 'Piskopi', 15 August, and Our Lady 'Myrtidiotissa', 24 September, at Kamari.*
*- The Purification of the Virgin, 2 February, at Oia.*
*- St John's day, 29 August, at Perissa, where local fava, olives, wine and bread are offered to all present.*

## SPORTS

*The main sport that one enjoys on Santorini is of course swimming. Wind-surfing equipment can be rented at Kamari. Santorini is also a wonderful place for hiking. There are so many things to explore on this fascinating island, and walking is the best way to really get to know a place.*

## SHOPPING

*Local products worth buying on the island include the various kinds of Santorini wine - brusco, bordeaux, vinsanto, nychteri - tomato paste and sun-dried tomatoes, and split yellow peas (fava). There are also handicrafts, such as handwoven rugs (to order from the Rug-making School at Fira) and embroideries, etc. Other good buys are gold jewellery and paintings by Greek and foreign artists, many of whom have taken their inspiration from Santorini's striking scenery and architecture.*

## WHAT ELSE YOU SHOULD KNOW

*Fira and Oia both have OTE (Greek Telephone Organisation) centres, where you can make local and long-distance telephone calls and send telegrams anywhere in the world. OTE Fira, 22.399 OTE Oia 71.242. Open from October - 15 June from 07.30-22.00 and from 16 June - 30 September from 07.30-24.00 Closed at weekends. At Fira, Oia and Pyrgos there are post offices. There is a Health Centre at Fira (22.237), while rural clinics may be found at Emborio (81.126), Oia (71.227), Pyrgos (31.207) and Therasia (23.191). Fira has several pharmacies. All pharmacies are open from Monday to Friday (normal shop hours), while there is always one on duty on nights and weekends on a rotating basis.*

*There are petrol stations and autorepair shops at Fira, Kamari and Pyrgos. Akrotiri and Karterado also have autorepair shops. In Greece, apart from the movable holidays of Clean Monday (the beginning of Lent), Good Friday, Easter, and Easter Monday and Whitmonday, the following official holidays are celebrated:*

| Jan. | Mar. | May | Aug. | Oct. | Dec. |
|------|------|-----|------|------|------|
| 1,6  | 25   | 1   | 15   | 28   | 25,26 |

*Banking hours are Monday-Thursday: 08.00-14.00; Friday: 08.00-13.30. All petrol stations are open Monday-Friday from 07.00-19.00; Saturday from 07.00-15.00, while some are open in the evenings (until midnight) and on Sundays (07.00-19.00) on a rotating basis.*

## USEFUL TELEPHONE NUMBERS

*Area code for Santorini (22860)*
*Police station 22.649*
*Town Hall, Fira 22.231*
*Town Hall, Oia 71.228*
*GNTO 71.234, 71.016*

## HOTELS

| C | N/L | TEL. | BEDS |
|---|-----|------|------|
| **Fira or Chora (0286)** | | | |
| A | Atlantis | 22.232 | 42 |
| A | Villa Theoxenia (P) | 22.950 | 12 |
| B | Villa Renos (P) | 22.369 | 13 |
| B | Porto Fira (F.A.) | 22.849 | 14 |
| C | Antonia | 22.879 | 20 |
| C | Dedalos | 22.834 | 40 |
| C | Hellas | 22.782 | 27 |
| C | Erolia | 22.155 | 32 |
| C | Theoxenia | 22.740 | 20 |
| C | Kavalari | 22.455 | 39 |
| C | Kallisti Thira | 22.317 | 64 |
| C | Panorama | 22.481 | 34 |
| C | Pelikan | 23.113 | 34 |
| C | Porto Karras | 22.979 | 16 |
| D | Anatoli | 22.307 | 21 |
| D | Leta | 22.540 | 22 |
| D | Loukas | 22.480 | 35 |
| D | M.P. Apartments (F.A.) | 22.752 | 12 |
| D | Santorini | 22.593 | 46 |
| D | Tataki | 22.389 | 18 |
| D | Flora | 81.524 | 14 |
| E | Asimina | 22.034 | 26 |
| E | Vina | - | 22 |
| E | Thirasia | 22.546 | 33 |
| E | Keti | 22.324 | 17 |
| E | Kastris | 22.842 | 15 |
| E | Lignos | 23.101 | 15 |
| | | | |
| **Akrotiri (0286)** | | | |
| C | Akrotiri | 81.375 | 30 |
| C | Goulielmos | 81.615 | 54 |
| D | Paradisos | 81.352 | 28 |
| | | | |
| **Vothonas (0286)** | | | |
| B | Mediterranean Beach | 31.167 | 80 |
| C | Markisia | 31.583 | 31 |
| | | | |
| **Vourvoulos (0286)** | | | |
| B | Santorini Villas (F.A.) | 22.036 | 14 |
| | | | |
| **Emborio** | | | |
| D | Archaia Elefsina | 81.250 | 28 |

## HOTELS

| C | N/L | TEL. | BEDS |
|---|-----|------|------|
| **Exo Gonia (0286)** | | | |
| A | Nano (F.A.) | 31.001 | 18 |
| C | Makarios | 31.375 | 54 |
| | | | |
| **Imerovigli (0286)** | | | |
| A | Altana Apartments (T.F.A.) | 23.240 | 30 |
| A | Iliotopos (F.A.) | 23.670 | 17 |
| B | Angeliki (F.A.) | - | 7 |
| B | Arts Apartments (F.A.) | 23.528 | 10 |
| B | Kelly's (F.A.) | - | 6 |
| B | Skaros Villas (T.F.A.) | 23.153 | 13 |
| C | Thanos Villas (F.A.) | 22.883 | 31 |
| C | Haneymoon Villas (F.A.) | 23.058 | 20 |
| E | Katerina | 22.708 | 18 |
| | | | |
| **Kamari (0286)** | | | |
| A | Kallisti Villas (F.A.) | - | 20 |
| A | Belonia Villas (F.A.) | 31.138 | 26 |
| B | Delfinia (F.A.) | 31.302 | 36 |
| B | Iliachtida | 31.394 | 68 |
| B | Rivari Santorini (H & B) | 31.687 | 42 |
| B | Rousos Beach | 31.255 | 72 |
| B | Christos (G.A.) | - | 40 |
| C | Akis | 31.670 | 24 |
| C | Alkyon | 31.295 | 28 |
| C | Argyros (F.A.) | - | 30 |
| C | Argo | 31.374 | 33 |
| C | Artemis Beach | 31.198 | 54 |
| C | Astro | 31.336 | 68 |
| C | Avra | 31.910 | 35 |
| C | Vatos | 31.660 | 54 |
| C | Zefyros | 31.108 | 44 |
| C | Kamari Beach | 31.243 | 93 |
| C | Kapetan Yiannis (F.A.) | 31.154 | 30 |
| C | Kastelli | 31.122 | 20 |
| C | Matina | 31.491 | 52 |
| C | Orion | 31.182 | 41 |
| C | Poseidon | 31.698 | 60 |
| C | Tropical Beach | 31.789 | 43 |
| D | Acropol | 31.012 | 30 |
| D | Andreas | 31.692 | 63 |
| D | Aspro Spiti | 31.441 | 29 |
| D | Golden Sun | 31.301 | 30 |
| D | Blue Sea | 31.481 | 49 |

**Abbreviations:** **C**=Category, **N/L**=Name/Location, **Tel.**=Telephone number, **Beds**=Number of beds, **M**=Motel **P**=Pension,